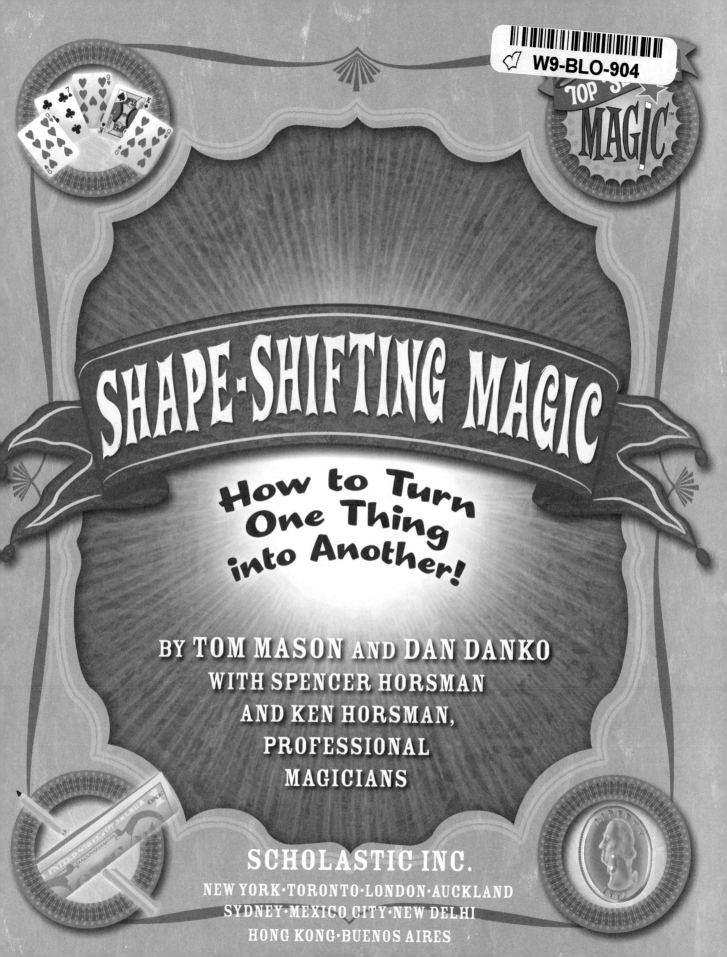

TOP
MAGIC

SHAPE-SHIFTING MAGIC

How to Turn One Thing into Another!

BY **TOM MASON** AND **DAN DANKO**
WITH **SPENCER HORSMAN**
AND **KEN HORSMAN**,
PROFESSIONAL
MAGICIANS

SCHOLASTIC INC.
NEW YORK·TORONTO·LONDON·AUCKLAND
SYDNEY·MEXICO CITY·NEW DELHI
HONG KONG·BUENOS AIRES

ISBN 0-439-90708-X

Copyright © 2006 by Scholastic Inc.

Design by Michaela Zanzani, Aruna Goldstein, Julia Melillo

Photography by Rocco Melillo

12 11 10 9 8 7 6 5 4 3 2 1   6 7 8 9 1 2/0

Printed in the U.S.A.

First Scholastic printing, October 2006

The publisher has made reasonable efforts to ensure that all the
material in this book is the writers' and magicians' original work. If any
errors have inadvertently been made, the publisher will take proper
corrective measures to acknowledge ownership
in future editions.

Table of Contents

Magical Morphing

Take a penny and turn it into a quarter. Start with the queen of diamonds and end up with the nine of hearts. Wave your hand to turn a blank book into a colored one. That's *transformation* magic, the art of changing one thing into something different—a different size, shape, color, or even a different object entirely! You're about to learn how to do these tricks and more.

One kind of transformation is the *switch*. This is where you secretly exchange one object for another without the audience seeing you do it. You'll get the hang of this when you perform the Incredible Shrinking Die trick.

Another kind of transformation is the *disguise*. With disguise, you make the audience think they're seeing something that's not really there! The Svengali cards are a good example of this. The audience believes you're holding a set of regular playing cards. But they're really seeing only the cards you want them to see.

You'll soon get the hang of the lingo as well as the tricks in this book, and then you'll be on your way to becoming a master transformer!

What's in Your Kit

SVENGALI DECK

This deck is specially designed to make magic happen automatically. You just have to learn some secrets about how to use it. Flip to page 19 to get started.

SHRINKING DIE

With the small die hidden inside the larger one, you can make the big die appear to shrink before your friends' eyes. All it takes is some sleight of hand you'll learn on page 10.

MAGIC COLORING BOOK

The pages of this book have a secret that can make colors appear or disappear when you flip through. Learn how to use it on page 6!

DOMINO CARD

The dots on this card look fixed, but you can move some of them around to make the number of dots change every time you flip over the card. On page 14, you'll learn the disguise that makes this trick possible.

THE TOP SECRET MAGIC WEB SITE

Check out the *Top Secret Magic* web site at www.scholastic.com/topsecretmagic for more magic tricks and tips. Just bring along this book's password: ShapeShift

The Invisible Crayons

COLOR AN ENTIRE BOOK WITHOUT CRAYONS!

Your Magic Coloring Book is a good example of a *gimmick*, or an object that looks ordinary but has a magic secret. The book has three sets of pages. Each set has tabs on the edges, and these tabs allow you to flip certain pages and skip the others. That makes the pages morph from blank...to black-and-white... to full color!

What You Need:
From Your Kit
✳ Magic Coloring Book

PERFORM!

1 Hold up the Magic Coloring Book so your audience can see it.

"I got this coloring book for my birthday. I really wanted a new video game and this seemed like such a lame gift. I'm way too old for coloring books."

Use this patter, or conversation, when you perform the trick!

Hold the spine of the book with your left hand. With your right hand on the bottom right corner, flip through the pages and show your audience the inside of the book. The pages will all be white.

"I thought my coloring book was even lamer when I opened it up and saw there weren't any pictures inside. But, I'm a magician, so I thought the least I could do was add some pictures to it."

Close the book and wave your hand over it. Throw in some magic words, too. (Try "Picasso, Da Vinci, Monet, Van Gogh, draw like there is no tomorrow!") You can even snap your fingers for added effect.

"And I was able to create some pretty cool pictures."

When you flip through the book this time, flip the pages from the top right corner. This is the tab for the black-and-white pages. As you flip, your audience will see black-and-white drawings on every page.

"How about that? And I only went to magic school, not art school! But I got tired of the black-and-white pictures. I wanted color, but I didn't want to sit down and color each page. Who has time for crayons when there's so much good stuff on TV?"

5

Now, you have your choice of fun things to do to bring color into the drawings. You can hold the book up to your forehead and transfer colors "from my brain!" You can also leave the book on the table and place both hands on it, transferring color through your fingertips. Or you can have the audience shout out their favorite colors for the book or ask volunteers to rub the colors from their clothes and hurl them at the book. (You can also think up your own ways to get color into the pages!)

"So I took all of my favorite colors—blue, green, yellow, red, orange—and transferred them to the book!"

TRICK TIP:

Having the audience participate gets them involved in the magic and makes them enjoy it even more! It's also a great bit of misdirection!

6

Now, flip through the book with your fingers at the middle of the right side. This is the tab for the color pages. All of the pictures will be in color. But you're not done yet. There's still more magic!

"If this were a normal coloring book, I'd be done. I could never color in it again. But with magic, I can use it again and again. Watch."

7

Shake the book in your hands, like you're shaking out all the pictures and colors.

"I want to get everything out. Out with the lines, out with the drawings, out with the colors. That should do it."

8

Now, pick up the book again and hold it exactly like you did in Step 2. Flip through the book with your right hand at the bottom. All the pages are blank again!

"Maybe this gift isn't so lame after all. But I still want a new video game!"

PRACTICE!

Work on holding the book and flipping the pages at the tabs so that it seems natural.

MAGIC HISTORY

In the mid-1800s, Signor Blitz, an English magician, began giving shows throughout the United States. When the Civil War broke out, he entertained thousands of Union troops. One of his tricks was taking an unsuspecting audience member's coat and dyeing it red. By the end of the trick, he had returned it to its original color!

The Incredible Shrinking Die

MAKE A LARGE DIE SHRINK

This is a classic misdirection trick. You have a small, solid die hidden inside a larger, hollow one. The audience follows the large die and really believes that it's been passed from one hand to the other. So when you open your hand to show them the small die, they'll think it's the same die they saw before, transformed into a new teeny-tiny size.

What You Need:

From Your Kit:
✳ The shrinking die—a large hollow die and a small die
Plus:
✳ A magic wand or a pencil

PREPARE...

1

Place the small die inside the hole of the larger die.

Cup your right hand slightly, and wedge the die between your middle finger and your little finger. The hole in the die should rest against your fingers.

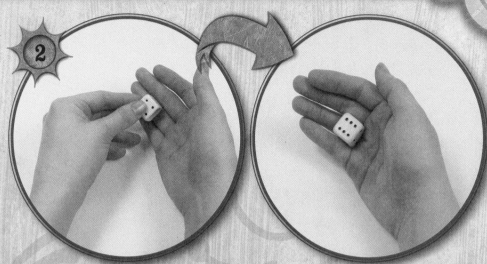

PERFORM!

"*Cleaning my room is a real problem for me because I've just got too much stuff. If I could just shrink it all, I could fit everything into a shoebox and my room would be clean in about ten seconds. Well, since I'm a magician, I decided to do just that!*"

Show the audience the large die in your right hand.

"*I'll show you what I'm talking about. Take this regular die, for example. It's just like the kind you'd use in any board game. Except that it's too big. I've got to shrink it for easier storage.*"

Show the audience that your left hand is completely empty.

"*Now, watch carefully. I'm going to pass the die to my left hand so I have my right hand free for my magic wand.*"

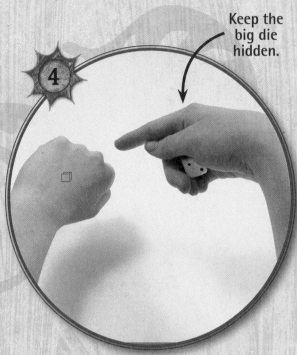

Keep the big die hidden.

As soon as the small die falls, immediately close your left hand over the small die so that no one can see it yet. Now, point to your left hand with the index finger of your closed right hand so that all attention is focused on your left. Your right hand still holds the large die.

"But it's going to need a little help."

Without letting the audience see what you're doing, tilt the large die with your right thumb and bring your left hand underneath to catch the small die. Keep the large die in your right hand.

"Now, the die is ready for shrinking."

PRACTICE!

Pretending to pass the large die from your right hand to your left is the hardest part of the trick and something that you should practice again and again so that it's as easy as blinking.

With your right hand still holding onto the hidden large die, pick up your magic wand or pencil.

"Now, for the last crucial step, I can achieve total shrinkage by passing the magic wand over my hand and saying the magic shrinking words..."

TRICK TIP:

You can involve the audience by asking one of them to blow on your left hand just before you pass the wand over it.

Wave the wand gently over your left hand and say some magic words, like, "Magic wand, hear my plea, make the die small like a flea!" Then open your left hand and let the small die roll out.

"And as you can see, the die has shrunk to its new, more convenient size! I bet I can have my whole room clean in a heartbeat!"

The Domino Effect

MAKE DOTS MULTIPLY AND DISAPPEAR!

This is a gimmick that requires some sleight of hand (secret hand movements that make magic happen). You've got a card with dots on it, like a domino. These dots look permanent, but some of them are really magnetic. This means that with a little sleight of hand, you can add or remove dots on each side of the card so that the number changes every time you flip the card over.

What You Need

From Your Kit:

✳ The domino card with four separate magnetic dots

PREPARE...

1

One side of your domino card has two printed dots. Place one magnetic dot directly over the center dot on this side.

2

The other side has five dots. On this side, place the remaining three magnetic dots on top of any of the printed dots.

"This next trick is sort of a math trick. You might be thinking, 'Oh, no, it's math.' But don't worry. Magic math is fun math! And besides, there are no grades to worry about."

Hold the card here.

1

FLIP

Hold up the card so that the two-dot side is facing the audience. Your right hand should be covering up the end dot so that only the middle dot is visible.

"How many ones are there in the number one?"

The audience now sees one dot (on the other side).

Wait for the audience's response.

"That's right. One. Now, if I were to multiply four times one, what would I get?"

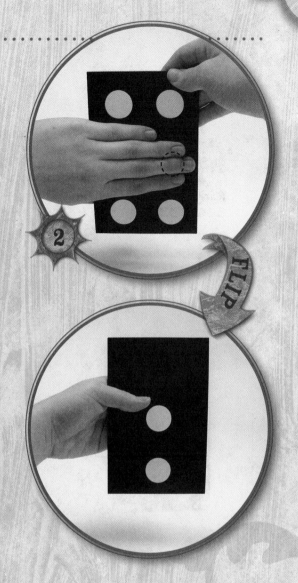

2

FLIP

Shift the card from your right hand to your left. The palm of your left hand should now be covering up the middle row dot so that only four dots show. Then, flip the card over so the five-dot side faces the audience.

"Correct again. One times four is four. But if I had four and lost two, how many would I have left?"

Wait for their response, then flip the card back to the two-dot side. As you do this, shift the card from your left hand back to your right hand. Your right hand should be holding the card at the empty end so that the two dots are showing.

"That's right. Four minus two is two. I have two dots now. But when it comes to magic math, my lucky number is really five."

Flip the card again, moving it from your right hand to your left hand. But before you flip, make sure that your left hand covers the empty space on the card so that all five of the printed dots are showing.

"And now that I've got my lucky number, we can move ahead to advanced magic math and some tougher questions."

5

FLIP

6

Hold the card flat with the five-dot side still facing the audience. Ask someone in the audience to wave his hand over the card. As your volunteer does this, slide the magnetic dot on the two-dot side, and create a third dot. Now, flip the card over to reveal the three dots.

"Now, here's the interesting thing. How many pigs make up the Three Little Pigs? That's right, three. And now I've got three dots on this side."

Now, ask a different audience member to wave a hand over the three dots. As someone does this, use your thumb to slide one of the magnetic dots on the five-dot side into place to create six evenly spaced dots.

"Now, I've got three dots on this side and there are two sides to the card, so what's three times two?"

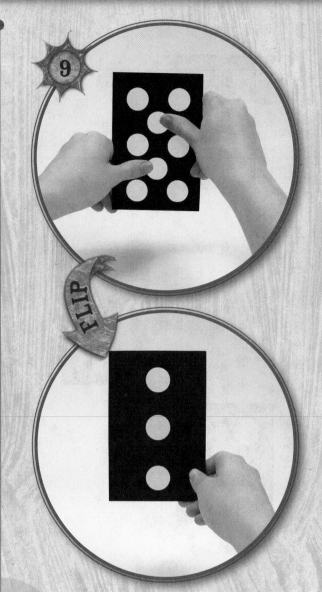

Flip the card over to reveal the six-dot side.

"That's right. Six."

Casually flip the card so that the audience can see both sides. There should be six dots on one side and three on the other. Stop with the three-dot side facing the audience.

"Okay, here's my final math question. Pick a number between seven and nine that isn't seven and isn't nine."

Wait for their response. While you're waiting, take the two remaining magnetic dots on the six-dot side, and with your thumbs, slide them into position between the two columns of three, to create a new column of dots in the middle of the card. Now, you have eight dots on the card. Flip the card over to reveal the eight-dot side.

"That's right, eight. I told you that magic math can be fun!"

PRACTICE!

The dots on your domino have to look evenly spaced. If they're uneven, your audience will suspect something's up!

The Secrets of Svengali

WHAT'S UP WITH THESE CARDS?

Grab the deck of Svengali cards from your kit. Open it up and sort through it. Seem a little funny? You're looking at a magician's secret: the Svengali cards.

Half the cards in your deck of Svengali cards all have the same face (the nine of hearts). The rest of the cards are just normal, random cards. What makes these cards perfect for doing magic tricks is that all of the nine of hearts cards are cut slightly shorter than the rest of the cards. That makes them behave differently from the longer cards, so you can control what your audience sees.

To do card tricks with the Svengali deck, you need to know a classic magician's move called the *riffle*. Here's how it works.

Before you do any trick with your Svengali deck, always make sure that it's in order. Every other card should be a nine of hearts, alternating with the random cards.

To do a forward riffle, first make sure that the back card is a nine of hearts and the front card is not. Then, put your thumb at the front of the deck and pull it backward. All of the cards will appear to be different.

To do a backward riffle, first make sure that the front card is a nine of hearts. Then start with your thumb at the back end and pull it forward. All the cards you'll see will be the nine of hearts.

Once you've nailed the riffles, forward and back, you're ready for some Svengali card transformations.

The Deck of Threes

TRANSFORM A DECK OF THE SAME CARDS INTO A REGULAR DECK!

With your Svengali deck, almost anything is possible. You'll show your friends that all the cards in your deck are the same. But with a magic tap or two, you'll make the deck morph before their eyes into a regular deck, with all different cards!

What You Need
From Your Kit:
* Svengali cards

PREPARE...

Arrange the Svengali cards so that they alternate between the short cards (the ones that all have the nine of hearts on them) and the long cards (the regular cards). For this trick, make sure the front card is a short one.

PERFORM!

"I bought these cards, but when I took them out of the package, I realized I probably should have spent my money on a CD or something. The cards I bought were all screwy."

1 Fan the cards, facedown, to the audience, to show that they are regular cards.

"Check 'em out. They look like regular cards."

Do a backward riffle to show the nines.

"But the printer obviously made a huge mistake. All the cards are the same! I'd just bought a whole bunch of the nine of hearts!"

Do a front riffle to show the audience that the cards are now different.

"Now, I've got some normal playing cards. And the cool thing is, if I don't want anyone borrowing my cards, I can change them back to nines!"

With the cards facedown, tap the pile two times.

"This is why it's great to be a magician. I can't fix a flat tire on my bike, but I can fix a deck of cards."

Tap the top of the deck two times, then do a backward riffle to show the nines again.

Memory Mess-Up

CHANGE A CARD
INTO A DIFFERENT CARD!

Show your audience the top card on your deck and ask them to remember it. Put it back and ask them to tell you what it was. Pull it off again and it'll be different! Did your magic card deck mess up their memories—or is the top card a shape-shifting card?

What You Need

From Your Kit:
✷ Svengali cards

PREPARE...

Arrange the Svengali cards so that they alternate between the short cards (the ones with the nine of hearts on them) and the long cards (the regular face cards), making sure that the front card is a long one and the back card is a short one.

PERFORM!

"This deck of playing cards really messes with people's minds. Let me show you what I mean."

1

Place the deck of cards on the table in front of you.

"It looks like an ordinary deck. But there's something funny about it."

2

Press down with your index finger to keep the two cards together.

With your thumb at the bottom of the deck and your middle finger at the top, lift the top two cards of the deck as if they were one. (In magician's slang, this is called a *double lift*.) Since the top card is slightly shorter and the second card is slightly longer, this will be easy. Tilt them toward your audience so they can see the face of the longer card.

"Look at this card. You don't have to tell me what it is, but remember it."

3

Replace the two cards facedown on top of the stack of cards. Then ask your audience to count backward from ten to clear their minds.

"Let's see if you remember what card it was. Everybody shout it out."

4

This time, slide just the top card off the top of the deck and show it to your audience.

"Sorry, everyone. You all remembered it wrong! But don't feel bad—I think this deck screws up people's memories. Nobody can ever remember their card!"

The Calling Card

TRANSFORM ANY CARD INTO ONE SELECTED BY THE AUDIENCE!

After someone in your audience picks a card and hides it in the deck, you won't find that card. Instead, you'll transform another card into the one that was picked. Or at least, that's what you'll make your audience think!

What You Need

From Your Kit:
* Svengali cards

Plus:
* A volunteer
* A magic wand (optional)

PREPARE...

Arrange the Svengali cards so that the cards alternate between the short cards (the ones with the nine of hearts on them) and the long cards (the regular face cards). Make sure the front card is a long card.

PERFORM!

"All right, I've got a deck of cards here."

1

Fan out the cards facedown to show the audience.

2 Square the cards up, and then do a forward riffle to show that they are all different.

"And I'm going to need a volunteer to help me."

3 Pick a volunteer from the audience.

"As I flip through the deck, I want you to tell me when to stop."

4 Slowly do a forward riffle until the volunteer says to stop.

"This is the card that you selected without any help from me."

Take the bottom half of the cards (the ones you already riffled through) and put them on the table. Point to the card that the volunteer has "selected"—the top card on that pile. Because of the forward riffle, the last card that landed will always be a short card, which means your volunteer's card will always be a nine of hearts.

"Pick up the card, look at it, and memorize it. But don't let me see it, and don't tell me what it is! When you're done, put it back."

After your volunteer returns the card to the pile of cards on the table, place the remainder of the cards facedown on top of the pile and neaten the deck so it's perfectly square.

"Your card is now lost, like Mary's little lamb, somewhere back in the deck."

Placing your thumb at the bottom of the deck and your middle finger at the top, press down slightly with your index finger as you slowly lift up about a third of the deck. This lifting method makes sure the top card on the stack you're leaving behind will be a nine of hearts.

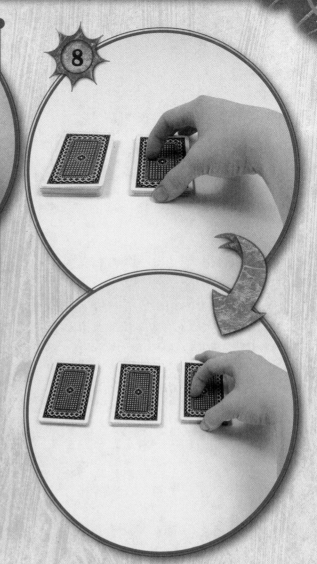

Set the cards you lifted on the table. Then lift up another portion of cards in the same way and set both remaining stacks on the table. A short card will now be on top of each stack.

"Now, please point to one of those piles."

PRACTICE!

Practice splitting the deck into three piles so the top cards are always the nine of hearts.

After your volunteer points to one pile of cards, combine the two unselected piles into a stack and add the pile that was selected to the top.

"You know that your card is in there somewhere. And I know it's in there somewhere, too. And I know what you're thinking. You're thinking that I'm going to find that card for you. Well, I'm not. That's way too hard."

"You see, I never was very good at finding a card in the middle of a deck. It's way easier for me to just change the top card into the one you selected."

Pick up the top card, and show the audience the nine of hearts.

"And is this the card you selected?"

Wave your magic wand or your hand over the cards and say a magic word.

❧ Short Forces ❧

There's no such thing as freedom of choice in magic. You're the magician and you're in control—even when the audience thinks they're calling the shots. The short cards in your Svengali deck are also known as *force cards*. Because they're shorter than the regular cards, you can control them and force the audience to choose one of them, while making it seem like the audience has a free choice or has chosen a card at random.

The String Doctor

TRANSFORM TWO PIECES OF STRING INTO ONE!

This is a tricky little trick. You're fooling the audience into thinking that two loops twisted in the middle of a long piece of string are really the ends of two different pieces of string. When you get rid of the loops by rubbing the string between your hands, the audience believes you've transformed the two pieces of string into one long piece!

What You Need:

* A ball of white cotton string that's made up of twisted strands
* Scissors
* A volunteer or two

 **PREPARE...**

1 Cut off about three feet of string from the ball.

2 Near the middle of the string, separate the strands and pull to create inch-long loops on either side.

3

Twist these loops in the direction they naturally want to go and pull at them with your fingers until they look like the ends of a piece of string.

With your fingertips, cover up the spot where the two loops separate from the main piece of string. When you hold this "joint," it should really look like you have two separate strings.

4

PERFORM!

"It was really windy yesterday, and I wanted to have some fun outside. So, I borrowed my little brother's kite without asking."

1

With the joint hidden between your finger and thumb, show your "strings" to the audience.

"The wind was really strong, though. It pulled on the kite hard and I almost couldn't hold on. Just when I thought I had it under control, the kite string broke."

PRACTICE!

Practice separating the string and positioning the strands so that the rigged joint is almost invisible. Try to find just the right angle at which to pinch the joint between your fingers so that no one can see the rigged joint. Use a mirror to find the angle that works best for you.

Let the ends of the string dangle across your palm.

2

"Now, I don't want to get in trouble for messing up my brother's kite, so I'm going to repair the string. Thanks to magic, I've become a professional string doctor."

Use your free hand to give one of the real ends to one of your volunteers. Give the other real end to your other volunteer. (If you only have one helper, give that person a real string end for each hand.) Keep pinching the two fake ends and have your volunteers pull their ends so the string is tight.

3

"Now, hold that tight, okay? You're like my surgical paper clip."

Bring your left hand under the string and quickly put your right fist over the fake ends. Gently rub your fist back and forth over the center of the string. You should feel the fake ends blend together.

4

"And now, we begin the operation. First I'll gently massage the string so that it feels better. This relieves any pressure and lets the string relax. Next, I'll say the magic words: Clamp, scalpel, sponge, I.V....let the string survive my surgery!"

Open your fist— your string is now all in one piece. You've "repaired" it!

5

"There, the operation was a success. We have a new piece of string that's ready to be reattached to my brother's kite. And no one will ever know! Until I send my brother the hospital bill."

Look Sharp!

TRANSFORM A DOLLAR INTO A SUPER-SHARP SWORD!

A dollar bill is pretty strong, especially if it has your hand to help it. In this trick, you'll pretend to cut a pencil in half with a dollar bill. You can make your friends think your magic has morphed the dollar bill into a super-sharp sword, when really, it's your fist that's breaking the pencil.

What You Need

* A dollar bill
* An unsharpened pencil
* A volunteer

 **PERFORM!**

"A dollar doesn't look very strong. It's easy to fold, and you can even tear it. But thanks to magic, I can transform a dollar bill into a sword. It'll still look the same, but you'll believe me when I use it to chop a pencil in half."

 Borrow a dollar bill from someone in the audience. If you have a large crowd, you can make a big deal out of finding "just the right dollar."

Fold the dollar in half the long way. Lay the bill against a table and slide your thumb along the fold to make a sharp crease.

"Folding a dollar like this is what makes it sharp. The crease has to be just right: sharp enough to chop through the pencil, but not so sharp that I cut myself."

Pick up the creased dollar and slice it through the air a few times, as if you were a Samurai warrior. Study the dollar carefully, as though you're checking for flaws. Run your thumb along the dollar's edge to test its "sharpness."

"That feels pretty sharp to me. I think the transformation is complete. Now, I need a volunteer from the audience to help me out."

Give the pencil to your volunteer, and make a fuss over the way he or she holds it. Adjust the pencil a couple of times, "just to be sure." Act like it's still not right and take the pencil back, showing your volunteer exactly how to hold it (palms up, as shown).

"The real trick is the proper placement of the pencil. Every pencil has a spot that's perfect for chopping with a dollar bill, and the trick is to find it."

 Make sure your volunteer's hands are at the very ends of the pencil and that the volunteer is holding it very tightly.

"Now, grip the pencil tightly, and hold your hands firmly. This dollar feels pretty sharp, and I'd hate for your new nickname to be 'Nine-Fingers.'"

 Holding the dollar between your thumb and index finger, slice it through the air a couple more times. You're ready to chop. Study the pencil—the audience will follow your lead.

"Shhh. Everybody be very quiet. Pencils can sense danger."

Now, slice the dollar down hard onto and past the pencil. Surprise! Nothing happens. Pretend it was supposed to work. Look at the pencil. Look at the dollar. Maybe even adjust the pencil slightly.

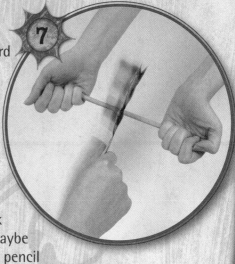

"Hmmmm. Something's not right. The dollar was supposed to chop the pencil in half. This is one tough pencil!"

8 Get ready again, and repeat the chopping action with the dollar. But this time, raise the dollar even higher, and bring it down even harder. The dollar will smack the pencil again, and once again, nothing will happen.

"Well, this is just crazy. Who gave me this dollar? Where did you get it?"

Raise the dollar way above your head now. Let the audience think you're really going to try harder now. You want to create a lot of

momentum with your swing. Now, slice the dollar past the pencil with a nice karate-type power yell. But this time, instead of bringing the dollar down onto the pencil, you're going to chop the pencil with your *fist*. SNAP! The pencil breaks. You should be able to do this fast enough so that the audience (and your volunteer!) never sees what happens. They'll really believe that the dollar finally cut the pencil in half.

"The dollar has done it! A pencil chopped in half by the power of a dollar bill!"

10 Now, hand the dollar back to the person who gave it to you, but make a show of unfolding it so it's now "safe."

"Be careful where you spend that. You don't want anyone to get hurt."

PRACTICE!

Buy a big box of pencils and practice breaking them with a friend beforehand so you know just how much force you need. It might be more than you expect.

Not-So-Honest Abe

TURN A PENNY INTO TWO DIFFERENT COINS!

This is a classic switch. You've got three coins, two of them hidden behind a penny. You move the penny to the back and make it look as if you're changing the penny into a quarter and a nickel.

What You Need

✶ Three coins: a penny, a nickel, and a quarter

2

PREPARE...

1

Pinch the nickel and the quarter between your thumb and index finger, a little ways back from your fingertips.

Audience View

Place the penny in front of them, facing out, and pinch it between the tips of your thumb and index finger. Hold your hand up to a mirror. You should only be able to see the penny and not the other two coins behind it. It sounds crazy, but it works!

PERFORM!

"Everyone wants to make more money. You could put it in the bank, try the stock market, or even gamble. But with magic, I can start with a little bit of money, and I guarantee you that I can get a whole lot more!"

Show the penny to the audience. The nickel and the quarter should be hidden behind it. If you keep your hand at the audience's eye level, they won't see the nickel and the quarter.

"Take this penny. It's got good old Abe Lincoln on the front, but it sure can't buy much."

Show your empty left hand to the audience. They now believe that the only thing in either of your hands is the penny.

"So I'm going to take this penny and turn it into thirty cents. That's better than you can do at any bank!"

Move your left hand toward your right hand. The index fingers and thumbs of both hands should point toward each other. Keep your hands level with the audience's eye level, or you'll give away the trick!

"Money multiplication isn't that difficult. It all depends on where you keep your money."

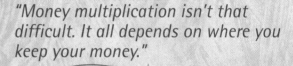

Bring your left thumb in front of the coins and push the penny to the left in line with the other two coins.

"I like to keep my money in my hands, because my hands are magic."

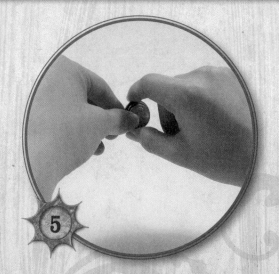

5

As soon as you do this, rotate the stack of coins so your audience sees the quarter in front.

"My magic hands can keep my money safe, but they can also increase my money."

Slide the nickel (with the penny hidden behind it) into your left hand, and keep holding the quarter with your right hand to show your audience that you've made thirty cents.

6

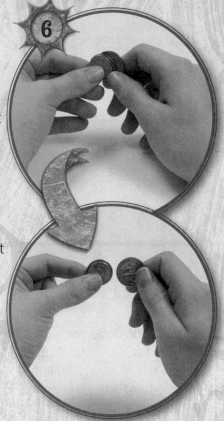

"Like now, for instance. It looks like my penny has disappeared, and now I've got thirty cents. That's a pretty good return on my magic investment!"

Point your palms out toward your audience to show that they're empty.

7

"I'd be more than happy to store any of your money in my magic hands as well!"

TRICK TIP:

Be careful when you put the three coins away. You don't want the audience to see that you still have the penny!

PRACTICE!

Every part of the trick depends on handling the coins smoothly. Make sure you can do each step smoothly and confidently, or else your audience will suspect something's fishy!

The Recycled Tree

GROW A TREE FROM NEWSPAPER!

After a tree gets made into paper, it can never be a tree again—or can it? With a little magic, anything is possible. In this trick, you'll make a paper tree seem to grow right before the audience's eyes.

What You Need
* Two full-page sheets of newspaper
* Scissors

PREPARE...

Tear the newspaper sheets in half and discard one half, leaving you with three pieces of equal size.

PERFORM!

"You already know that trees get turned into newspapers. But I'll bet you can't turn a newspaper back into a tree. Fortunately, I'm a magician, so I'm going to show you a bit of home-recycling magic to make that happen!"

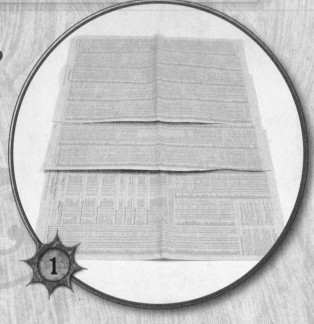

Lay one of the half sheets on the table with the long edge facing you and place a second half sheet on top of it, overlapping about halfway. Place the third piece of newspaper behind that one, again overlapping halfway.

Roll the papers into a tube. Start with the piece closest to you, and roll away from you. Then hold the paper tightly so it can't unroll.

"In order to grow a tree, you have to plant the seeds. That's what these sheets of newspaper are—the seeds of my tree."

Start at the top and cut straight down the center of the tube. Stop when you reach the middle. Cut four or five more slits down the tube, stopping at the middle each time.

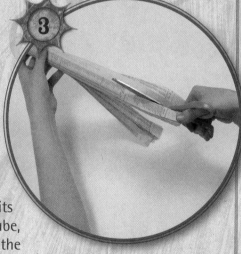

"Look—our tree is starting to sprout a few leaves and a couple of branches."

TRICK TIP:

Use the Sunday comics section or even some wrapping paper to make a more colorful tree.

Reach into the center of your roll of newspaper to grab onto one of the center "branches," and slowly pull it up to make a nice, bushy tree!

"Now, I'm going to plant this in my front yard, and grow some more newspapers!"

PRACTICE!

Practice pulling on a branch to get your tree to grow. You'll need to let the newspaper move through the hand that's holding onto the "trunk" so the paper can telescope outward as the tree extends.

The Runaway Dogs

MAKE FOUR JACKS MAGICALLY APPEAR AT THE TOP OF A DECK OF CARDS!

As you tell your audience a story about runaway dogs, you'll scatter four jacks through the deck—or that's what your audience will think you're doing! Really, the jacks stay on top the whole time. It works because of some sneaky secret cards that your audience never knows about.

What You Need:
* A regular deck of playing cards
* A magic wand or pencil

 **PREPARE...**

Remove the four jacks from the deck and place them on top of any three other cards, all faceup. Your audience should never see the three cards that are now on the bottom of this stack. You'll make them think you've only got four cards there, and they won't have a chance to count.

Hide the three bottom cards from your audience.

"I like animals, but sometimes they can really get out of control. Once I had to take care of my neighbor's dogs. She told me they were good dogs, but I think she was just saying that so I'd agree to help out."

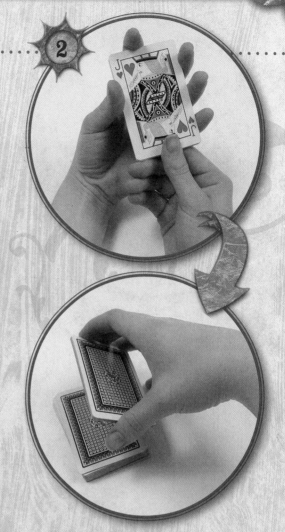

2

1

The three non-jacks are hidden under here.

Hold the seven cards in your right hand, faceup. Fan the jacks out to the audience, but make sure that the three non-jacks are hidden so the audience doesn't see them.

"I didn't think it was going to be a difficult job until I found out she had four dogs: Rover, Rex, Fido, and Constantinople."

Square up the seven cards, turn them facedown, and place them on top of the rest of the facedown deck. Move smoothly with the cards, and the audience will think you added just four cards instead of seven.

"After I fed them, I put them in the backyard for the night, but apparently, I didn't latch the back gate like I was supposed to. These dogs raced right past me out of the backyard. By the time I realized what had happened, they had run away. This wasn't going to be my day."

4 Take the next card from the top and slide it facedown into the middle of the deck. Let it stick out, too.

"Rex ran down to the local mall."

5 Take the next top card, and slide it in near the top of the deck. You've now removed the non-jacks from the top of the deck.

"Fido went across the street."

Pick up the facedown deck in your left hand. Keep it tilted downward just a little bit. Pick up the top card (which is one of the non-jacks), and keeping it facedown, slide it in about a dozen cards from the bottom of the deck. Let the card stick out about an inch or so.

"Rover ran the farthest, all the way to the edge of town."

6 Now, show the top card to the audience. It's one of the jacks. Keep it on top of the deck, and let it stick out the same as the other three cards. The audience will believe that the other cards sticking out are jacks as well.

"I managed to catch Constantinople by the collar and bring him back. But what about the others?"

Wave your magic wand over the deck. One at a time, turn over the top four cards. The jacks are all back.

"Constantinople. Fido. Rex. Rover. All four dogs are back home. Good thing I'm a magician."

Very slowly, so that everyone can see, square up the deck. Tap it twice with your magic wand or pencil as you speak.

"I had my magic wand, so I used some special dog magic to call them home: 'Rover, come on over! Rex, you're next! Fido, don't hide-o!'"

TRICK TIP:

Make up your own story to go with the trick. You can use runaway monkeys, or escaped robots, or lost socks!

The Crybaby Quarter

MAKE A QUARTER CRY!

Does the quarter really cry? Only if you're mean to it. This sleight-of-hand trick starts with a wet tissue ball hidden behind your ear. Then, you sneak the tissue behind the quarter, and when you squeeze out the water, it looks like the coin is crying.

What You Need:
* A piece of tissue
* A quarter

 **PREPARE...**

Tear off a corner of the tissue and wet it. Form it into a small wet ball and hide it behind your right ear. Then, start the trick right away—you don't want the ball to dry out.

 **PERFORM!**

"A quarter is made of pretty tough stuff. You can't bend it, you can't break it. But a quarter isn't really that tough. I can use a bit of magic to make it cry like it just saw a sad movie."

Ask someone in the audience to lend you a quarter.

"I hold in my hand a normal quarter."

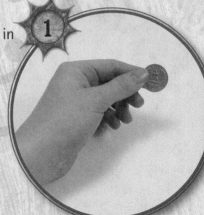

Study the front of the quarter as if you're looking carefully at George Washington's face.

"But this quarter is dirty. Good ol' George Washington has some gunk stuck in his eye and it's clogging his tear ducts. I've gotta clean that out first."

Your right hand is grabbing the tissue from behind your ear.

Bend your right arm and raise it so that your right hand goes behind your right ear. Rub the quarter up and down your left forearm from your wrist to your elbow. While you talk, your right hand grabs the tissue ball behind your ear and holds it between your fingers, hidden from the audience.

"Rubbing the quarter against my arm will wipe out the gunk and open his tear ducts."

PRACTICE!

Use a mirror to practice moving the wet tissue ball from behind your ear to behind the quarter, without exposing the tissue ball. The mirror is also a good way to figure out how big the tissue ball should be. And make sure the ball is wet enough for the water to drip out.

Now, bring down your arm. As your hands come together, secretly slide the wet tissue ball behind the coin.

"That should be enough."

Squeeze the tissue from behind the coin, and hold your other hand underneath the coin. Water will drip from the hidden tissue. Your quarter is "crying!"

"Maybe instead of George Washington, they should put a picture of a baby on the quarter. What do you think?"

The Buck Stops Here

MAGICALLY TURN A DOLLAR BILL UPSIDE DOWN!

This is a very good example of a disguise. The dollar really is turning around. The folding and unfolding distract the audience as the dollar is turned in the opposite direction!

What You Need:

✴ A dollar bill

PERFORM!

"I'm not what you'd call organized. My room is messy. I have a hard time finding my favorite shirt sometimes. And I don't always put my things away."

1 Hold the bill so that the front faces you and the back is to the audience.

"I'm even like that with my money, like this dollar that I'm holding right-side up."

2 Fold the dollar bill down toward you lengthwise.

3 Bring the right-hand edges toward you and over onto the left-hand edges to fold the bill in half widthwise.

"I don't keep my money nice and neat in my wallet, but I do fold it up and put it in my pocket. And I try to have all my bills facing the same way. But I have this one dollar bill that has a mind of its own."

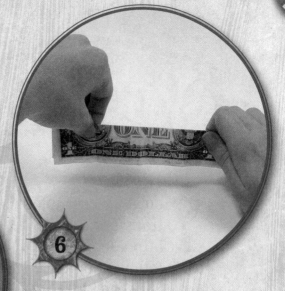

Fold the dollar bill the same way again, taking the right side over the left.

"Every time I take my money out of my pocket, this particular dollar is always upside down. I turn it right-side up and put it back in its place. But the next time I get my money out, it's upside down again."

Unfold the far right side to the left.

"I even asked my friend to try it for me. He folded it just like I did, and then tried unfolding it, to see if it did the same thing for him."

Slowly and dramatically, unfold the bill toward you lengthwise. The bill is now upside down, with the back of the bill again facing the audience.

"Wouldn't you know it? Every time he unfolded the dollar, it had turned itself upside down again!"

Unfold both ends on the far left side (the side closest to the audience) to the right.

You've Transformed!

You've just completed your most amazing transformation of all—yourself! You've morphed into a magician who can handle switches, disguises, misdirection, and more. And with those tricks up your sleeve, you can make just about anything morph before your audience's eyes—dice, dominos, coloring books, playing cards, and lots more.

The secret to great transformation magic is to keep transforming *different* things. Shrink that die too many times and the audience might figure out what's going on. This is especially important with your Svengali cards. You learned three different tricks, but perform them each for different audiences. Otherwise, your friends might wonder why the nine of hearts shows up in every single trick!

Keep practicing your sleight of hand and your patter until your shape-shifting magic looks natural. And stay tuned for the next *Top Secret Magic* book—the secrets to a whole new type of magic await you!